$R^{u^{n}}$

Run

Ted Jonathan

NQY Books™

The New York Quarterly Foundation, Inc.
New York, New York

NYQ Books™ is an imprint of The New York Quarterly Foundation, Inc.

The New York Quarterly Foundation, Inc.
P. O. Box 2015
Old Chelsea Station
New York, NY 10113

www.nyq.org

First Edition

Set in New Baskerville

Cover Design by Amy Foster

Author Photo by i. r. schwinnman

Library of Congress Control Number: 2016931043

ISBN: 978-1-63045-023-6

Run

Acknowledgments

Thanks to the editors of the following journals and anthologies who published some of the poems in this collection:

Chiron Review, Dead Flowers, The Iconoclast, Lyre Lyre, Mas Tequila Review, Misfit Magazine, Nerve Cowboy, Paddlefish, Paterson Literary Review, Pedestal, Ray's Road Review, Skidrow Penthouse, Slant, Sugar Mule, Third Wednesday, Trajectory, Two Hawks Quarterly

It's Animal but Merciful: (great weather for MEDIA, anthology, 2012)

The Understanding between Foxes and Light: (great weather for MEDIA, anthology, 2013)

Thank you to Raymond Hammond for publishing this book. Thank you to Amy Foster for her cover design. Thank you to Tony Gloeggler, Michael A. Flanagan, and L. S. for their feedback on poems in progress. I've become pretty good at finding the right people.

And thank you to the late great William Packard for everything.

Contents

for Amanda, Amy, and Barbara

Dominion

I live in the basement
but—like you—have rights
to the sky, so I hang El Greco's
"Toledo" on the wall facing
my easy chair. Swirling
blue-gray clouds, dark
ominous sky. Man's fate
hanging by a thread. Flood.
Okay. As long as it's not
only me. But the sky changes.
Alongside "Toledo," I hang
Magritte's "The Dominion
of Light." Nicely aligned puffy
white clouds soften a bright
blue sky. The paintings remained
until I, like George Jefferson,
moved on up. Atop a steep
as-a-wall NJ cliff high up

on floor 33. Here in the sky,
on a bright-blue day, I see
the unglamorous northern
Manhattan skyline across
the vast Hudson River,
and beyond, the enormous
blimp looms dumbly over
Yankee Stadium. Deeper into
the Bronx, 13-year-old me
sits at one end of our old
living-room sofa and my father
at the other. He's watching
another war documentary on TV.
I eye the heavy metal base table
lamp. The one I'll use to bash
in the back of his head, next time
he raises a hand against my mother.
If ever I'd had the chance.

Poe Park

It had nothing to do with kicks.

Just the need to slow the invasive
train of repetitious thoughts rolling
unrelentingly through my head.

Outside of Poe Park I'd usually
be able to cop downers.
This hot night was no exception.
Done deal.

Stepped into the empty park to swallow
the promise of stupor.

Block-long, it was mostly concrete
and broken glass. It was 1976, and
I couldn't care less that within a mile,
landlords were torching buildings
into cash and the Yanks were making
a pennant run.

Cut across the park...

At the far end, sitting on the stoop of an
old white-frame cottage, was a tattered
lone soul playing guitar and singing. Long
limp blond hair hid much of his face, as he
sang Simon & Garfunkel's *El Condor Pasa*.
"I'd rather be a hammer than a nail..."

I hadn't seen him in ten years (when we
sat shoulder to shoulder in 7th grade), but
here was my former classmate—Ivar Kertes—
singing to a squirrel. Ivar, who could swing
on clarinet and run like a Cadillac.

In class, to get my attention he'd gently
elbow me. "Look intelligent Theodore,"
he'd say, straight-faced, as he fingered
imaginary scraggle on his chin, to affect
serious contemplation.

No longer Ted, but Theodore, I'd follow.
Then we'd face the teacher.

Rivet our eyes on him as though our very
lives depended on it and scratch our hairless
twelve-year-old chinny-chin-chins. Every
day for one or two minutes straight, we
looked intelligent.

I heard Ivar had gone schizo.

The downs melted my mind slow. Running
into Ivar, I momentarily forgot how scared
I was—not of Ivar, but of my own mind.

Waited for him to break before warmly saying,
"Hey!"

He did a protrude-lower-lip-out-and-blow-air-up
move, blowing his hair from his face. Armageddon-
eyed, he smiled recognition.

Slurring, I asked, "Is it true your old man
was a Ukrainian Nazi collaborator and trained
your mutt to salute when he said *sieg heil?*"

"To hell with him!" said Ivar. "He's dead."

After assuring him that I'd buy another bottle,
I reached over and threw back a heartening hit
of his Wild Irish Rose. He plunged back into

"I'd rather be a hammer than a nail / Yes I would /
If I cou—ou—ould / I surely wou—"

"Ivar man!" I interrupted. "That hammer and nail
shit sucks."

Resting the guitar at his side, he raised the Wild
Irish to his lips and drained a long red swig.
Tossed the bottle *splattercrash* onto concrete.

"Theodore," he said, "it's the melody I love."

"I do too. It's an old Peruvian folk tune.
Simon stuffed it with hammers and nails."

Ivar rose to his feet.

As though he were unveiling the Temple of
Artemis, with a sweeping gesture of his right
arm he presented the old white-frame cottage.
Awestruck, he held the pose for a moment.

I beheld the cottage. Flaked clapboard paint
and broken multi-pane windows. Heavy chains,
secured by 2 padlocks, festooned the 2 front doors.

"Do you know who lived here, Theodore?"

"Yeah. The poet Poe."

"Yeah," he affirmed. "The poet Poe. The Bronx
was country then. And this was a fine little farm-
house. Poe rented it. Lived here with his wife. She
died young. Here, of TB. He lives on. I AM HE!"
As the sun set, he launched into *The Raven*.

Out on my feet, I fell to my knees.

Polio

Popeye had his spinach. Reagan had his jelly beans. Elvis had his curled lip. Popeye was strong to the finish. Sinatra had his rat-pack. The Situation's got his six-pack. The Kennedys had Marilyn. Travis Bickle had his mohawk. W had his Godless smirk. One poet invokes Miles Davis in an attempt to cop some cool. The emperor's got no clothes. Mojo died with Muddy Waters. Supercalifragilisticexpialidocious. Bukowski had his wine & his muse. Ali had the heart of a lion. The Clash had "White Riot." Shrewdest guy I ever met often played the fool. Leadbelly had Stagger Lee. Lenny Bruce had his smack & shtick. *Kill or be killed.* Jonas Salk invented the cure and refused to accept a cent.

Tractus

for William Packard

The nightly ritual (washing down valium with
Heineken), while intently watching The Arsenio
Hall Show (muted) no longer knocked me out.
Turned to the wall for what crawled out my soul…

Knew I'd rather be dead,
than spend another day at the job.

Stopped showing up.

Took up poetry.

The teacher was a young woman. Everyone
seemed to know one another. They went around
the room for some kind of feelings check. No
talk of poetry. Broke into a cold sweat. Group
therapy? My turn, I passed. Finished the fight
I had with a guy coming in on the subway
when the teacher announced the end of class and
the one book required. Said it was by a colleague.
The title included the word *tractus*. On my way
out, I asked, "Will we be learning poetic devices?"
She replied, "You can do that on your own."
"Is that how you learned?" I asked. And didn't
wait for an answer.

I rode the unbridled guitar bursts of grunge king
Neil Young and wrote lyrics that sang. Another,
a la Randy Newman, jabbing needles into that what
needs needling. Cut costs like the dry cleaners and
cable. Dropped insurance. Read Coleridge and Buk.
Got a part-time job doing quality control at a Pez
factory. And wrote a song like no one but me.

Tried again.

In this man, even a half-wit could tell they sat
before a monumental teacher. Not because he had
the imposing stature of one who way back might've
played fullback or because of his gray beard
and great head of dark unkempt hair, but because
of his glaring vast knowledge and roaring laughter
of wakefulness. There was a cop, a supermodel,
and an astrophysicist in the class. A woman seated
up front peppered him with *daddy, daddy please notice
me* questions. He threw her out. It warmed my heart.
Here was my chance to get something right.

Reunion

You cried in class, when
President Kennedy was shot.
A cute girl, with red curls,
in a third-grade class filled
with smart kids whose moms
and dads made their dioramas.

I was put into that class, made
friends, felt nothing when
Kennedy was killed. You had
a crush on me. I was elected
class president. Maybe someday
you'd be my girlfriend.

So when I looked to see who,
in the car stopped for a red light,
was calling me, as I hung out
killing time on the Lydig Ave.
street corner of the Bronx
neighborhood that I'd never left,
I knew it was you. Even though
fifteen years had been snuffed.
"Hi Leslie," I said. "Ted, Ted-dy!"
she yelled, "I'm very late—phone-
book—Queens—Leslie Herman—
Herman—Herman! Phone me!"
And drove away.

At her apartment in Queens, she
said she'd gone to the state university
in New Paltz and left to hook-up
with the Moonies. That currently
she was temping. She got naked
and blasted a fart. Said she wanted
to suck my toes and looked to me
for her cue to start.

While I thought: my feet are
unwashed, I need more Tuinals,
did I run over that cop's foot
at the Whitestone Bridge tollbooth
after his open palm slammed
the hood of my borrowed car
and he ordered me to stop? Lighted
a Marlboro. Got up to leave. I can
only do it with whores.

The Turks

"Yes," said the driver of the nameless New Jersey bus.
"The last stop's 42nd and 8th in New York. Three dollars. Pay
when you get off." I stuffed my cash back into my pant pocket,
and considered taking the seat that was broken into chaise
lounge position of the converted school bus, before taking
a right-window seat in the middle. A lifetime of New York City
subway riding inured me from the remnant stench of unwashed
ass. The only other passenger was a well-groomed older man
seated on the other side on the aisle a couple rows in back
of me. To assure passengers that the dusky black-bearded
driver wasn't a terrorist, an American flag was affixed above
a stuffed Mickey Mouse seated on the driver's rear view mirror.
Mickey's legs blocked the mirror almost entirely. I slept…

until I was awoken by a booming two-way between the well-
groomed older man and a nondescript middle-aged man sitting
directly in front of me. They were speaking a foreign language.
I'd become immune to such rude loud conversations if I
could identify the language, but I couldn't recognize theirs.
And was about to tell the guy in front of me that I'd strongly
prefer not to hear them, but what calmly came out of my mouth
was, "What language are you speaking?" "Turkish," he replied.
"Oh," I said, "like the Ottoman Empire or immortal poet Nazim
Hikmet." In broken English, he sang the praises of his homeland.
Because I've spent well over 90% of my life pretending to listen
to what others are saying, I feigned listening while I drifted into
thinking of a girl who years back worked at Tower Records.

Her name was Fem and she too was Turkish. She was a painter
who worked in their classical music section. She said she only
liked music and art of the Baroque period, and was supposed
to have been born then. I wasn't sure when the Baroque period
was but liked what she said because modern times surely wasn't
working for me. Fem was a high-cheekboned snowflake, with dark

20

almond-eyes and flowing hair. An angel or a witch. When the bus
arrived at 42nd and 8th, I waited for the others to get off before
getting up and handing 3 bucks to the driver. He shook his head no,
gestured toward the street at the talkative Turk who just got off,
and said he'd paid my fare. As for Fem I'd asked her if she'd like to
go to the Metropolitan Museum with me. "I might," she said, smiling.

Quietism

No choice. Vocal cord paralyzed.
Only an exhausting stream of
a ghastly whisper. Something
from someone already dead. "I'm
a sick man! Please…" I'd wheeze
into the phone when working
the HMO. Otherwise, mouth shut.

Like when the feeder of pigeons,
my spacey longtime neighbor, Isis,
recoiled and said, "You look like hell!"
when we crossed paths in the hallway
upon my release from the hospital.
If I had my voice I would've said,
"May the dirty pigeons turn on
you and slowly peck you to death."

Stayed home. Reflecting. Consoled
myself that I'd rather be voiceless
than sightless. Then tried to trick God
into resurrecting my voice by praying
for the callous Isis. And swore I'd
remain a man of few words, except
for poetry readings.

On my way home from another useless
visit to the kindly speech therapist,
I decided to stand in the long line
for a Domino's Pizza grand-opening
giveaway. Two slices left when
the server hands the woman ahead
of me a slice. She hands it back, saying
she wants the other one. The bigger
one. Leaving me…Ordinarily, I
would've said something. Anything.

Home again. Reflecting. Beyond my-
self. Realized that the vanity plate
wasn't the most American of all things.
Had to be the laugh track or the idling
engine...The angelic drummer-girl
Karen Carpenter's singing was worthy
of Homer's Sirens... And the spirits
of the dead don't ride the wind. A year
passed. And then my voice returned.
Was it God's will? I was deeply grateful...
And then took it for granted.

No Evidence of a Tumor

"You got a nice dick," she says. Toy voice like a flute. The appraiser. Strokes it. Planet Ass in my face. HOT DIGGITY DOG ZIGGITY BOOM! But what's this *nice* shit? The way she says it, I know she means *nice* like you say after watching your team turn an around the horn double play. Or how I felt when I saw my next door neighbor's cockatoo fly out the window. She's a blunt, tough little nut, but I've got to…"Big enough?" "Just right," she says. And she knows dicks. Really. Night of many not so slight exquisite deaths. *Just right.* Two syllables. Delivered just right. Syllable for syllable, beating the eight uttered by the doctor years later after yet another surgery.

Decoder Poem

When they say,
I feel your pain.
They really mean—
Even your pain
is theirs to claim.

When they say,
Some things you
shouldn't
have to pay for.
They really mean—
They're scheming
24/7
to make you pay.

When they say,
There are two sides
to every story.
They really mean—
Whatever side you're on
they'll take the other.

When they say,
I've made peace with it.
They really mean—
They'll take it to the grave.

When they say,
Buy one get one free.
They really mean—
They've quadrupled
the price of one.

When they say,
their parents did
the best they could.

They really mean—
They would've
been better off
being brought up
in an orphanage.

When they say,
Fifty is the new forty.
They really mean—
They're pushing sixty.

When they say,
So sorry to hear that.
They really mean—
Your sorrow is
their sustenance.

When they say,
He's like family.
They really mean—
They're paying him less
than the minimum wage.

When they say,
Don't be a stranger.
They really mean—
They rue the day
you were born.

When they say,
No cause for alarm.
Consider suicide.

Grand Prix

The '71 2-door baby-blue
black hardtop Pontiac Grand
Prix was 10 years old, but had
low mileage and was mint
when I bought it for $1,000
from an old woman up in
Tarrytown, who only drove
it twice a week to and from
the A&P. Otherwise, she kept
the 400-horsepower Coke-bottle-
shaped muscle car with automatic
everything in her garage. I never
asked why she ever owned
such a car. I did know that I'd
struck gold. An enterprising guy
could easily double his money.
I wasn't enterprising. Nor was
I a car guy, and this was very
much a car guy car. But in my gut,
I knew it had to be mine.

Parked by the P.S. 105 Bronx
schoolyard, the very next day
I sat behind the wheel, next to
a drug dealer named—believe-it-
or-not—Paul Bunyan, who I got
on with okay but was a prick
and bully. On and on he went
about how much he loved
the Grand Prix. When a kid
on the street stared at the car
and us, Bunyan savored saying,
"What're you lookin' at, sonny?"
I revved the engine, which roared
a testicle-quaking riot. He got out
and looked back, unleashing
a shit-eating grin.

Blacked-out at a Long Island
disco. Myles took over the wheel
going home. By this time
the Grand Prix was plenty
dented from months of me
driving stoned: through
a garage door, into a subway
pillar, etc. Myles had mainlined
a speedball, had a glass eye,
no license, and used his left
foot for the brake, his right
for the gas pedal, and was coolly
resigned to an early death.
We couldn't find our way out
of an area where palatial homes
mocked us. From the back,
Myles' younger brother, Jay, said,
"Let's pull a Charles Manson."

Stoned, I drove to a singles
mixer in Manhattan. Hit it off
with a nurse named Ahuva.
Like the vacuum cleaner, she
said. Vacuum cleaner, indeed.
She was a ripe white pear,
and had a nice place on the Upper
East Side. Next morning I gave
the doorman a that's-right-I'm-
fucking-her-and-it's-not-costing-
me-a-penny-and-thanks-for-
holding-the-door-for-me-smiley,
good-bye.

But forgot where I parked.
Couldn't find the car. Clueless.
Hours later, the same forces

that protected while in the Grand
Prix delivered. At a red light,
a guy pulled up alongside of me.
Asked how much I wanted for it.
I said, $1,000. And that was that.
Or so I thought.

Because many nights, many years,
I'd dream, searching for my Grand Prix.
No longer though, I hate to say.

My Sister Tells Me

for Dr. Barbara R. Greenberg

After she told mom
old Ben of Ben's Hobby Shop
urged her and other little
girls to climb the ladder
and look at items shelved
highest so he could look
up their skirts, mom
marched in with her.

After she got caught
shoplifting Turkish Taffy
from Bib & Sam's street
corner candy store, mom
took her to Woolworth's
on White Plains Road,
bought her marbleized
pencils, so that she'd no
longer feel deprived.

After she told mom
2 girls at school snatched
her wooly white pom-pom
hat during recess and flung
it to and fro playing saloogie
mom told her what to say
to the bigger one. She did.
It didn't happen again.

She didn't have to tell me
how proud mom was when,
at age 9, she won the school
spelling bee. Or how proud
mom would've been had she
survived beyond her beloved
Basia Roza's tenth birthday,
to see her lop heads from
the hydra we call life.

The Paisley Shirt

I liked going to Fordham Road with my mom.
We'd take the 12A bus to the block-after-block
hustle-bustle Bronx shopping stretch. When I
was ten, my mother took me there, to Alexander's
department store, to buy me a couple of shirts
for the coming school year. The store was grand,
it had everything. But what I liked most of all
was being there with her. She was kind, pretty,
and young. She bought what we could afford, 2
bargain bin paisley shirts. Afterwards, we walked
a few blocks to the RKO Fordham to see "The Sound
of Music." But I can't say I liked the homely Miss
Hathaway of "The Beverly Hillbillies" look-alike
belting out how the "hills come alive."

When I wore one of the shirts to school, the jaunty
male teacher announced to the entire class that
another kid, Lucas Ortiz, and I were wearing identical
shirts, like he was shocked that 2 boys in the same
crowded working-class 4th grade Bronx classroom
would be sporting the same cheap shirt. The paisley
shirt my mother chose. Shielded by the fashion
faux pas, he pleasured in shaming us. My face flushed
red heat. Shame trumped rage but I blurted, fuck you.
And Lucas, who perhaps didn't even care about
the teacher's crack, had to outdo me, hurling a chair.
But I didn't blurt fuck you, and Lucas didn't hurl
a chair. Shame stuck to my gut, the shirt, to my back.

Elementary School

Squat & curl up
under desk should
the commies come
dropping bombs.

Men with cool
names like Vasco
De Gama were first
to sail straight to
India, and Ponce
De Leon, looking
for the fountain
of youth, was first
to set foot in Florida.

Johnny B. would
show off chomping
down chalk, Louis
could be tricked
into drinking piss.

We could watch
my Jew, Jack Ruby
shoot to death
the 3 named goon
who shot to death
our golden President
on live television

Boys in size-place
order, meant me
wanting to be taller.

When the father
of our country was
a boy he couldn't tell

a lie, and confessed
to chopping down
a cherry tree.

We warred against
the people of North
Vietnam on account
of a Domino Theory.

Mondays meant
white shirts & green
ties to assembly,
all of us singing
of stout hearted
men, who'd stand
shoulder to shoulder
& fight to the end…

It was cooler to like
The Byrds, dumb
"Mr. Tambourine Man,"
than Barbara Mason's
heady & soulful
"Yes, I'm Ready."

Plotnik could be hung
by his collar on a hook
and left there all day
in a closed closet.

Everyone had a right
to their own opinion.
And everyone had one.

Kill (2)

The music video. I don't care
who directs it. Although I know
it's not Kubrick.

The hoarder who lives below me,
before he kills me with his stench
arsenal of mothballs and decay.

Those who'd privatize social security.
Their families. Harvest all organs.
Piss on their bones.

That fat-ass plaque in Yankee Stadium's
monument park, dedicated to the team's
late swinish owner, Steinbrenner.

Those who try to sell us Mariah Carey
and Maggie Gyllenhaal as foxes. Or as
you might say, "hotties." But I won't.

Corporate interests & pedophiles.
Former first. If it's good for them—
it's bad for you. Real bad.

Any past or present reference
to Madonna as a diva.

The price-gouge cost
of generic stool softener
at the Good Neighbor Pharmacy
in Guttenberg, New Jersey.

The willfully ignorant.

The Rock and Roll Hall of Fame.
Turn it into a bingo parlor, a whore-
house, or a lottery superstore.

Any poet who, when giving a reading,
asks if he has time for one more.
Less is more. More or less.

Anyone who doesn't inherently
get the difference between
earning money and *making* it.

Anyone with perfect bleached white teeth
and tattoos. Unless they sport a facial tattoo.

Socialized medicine for elected officials.

Bagism.
Tagism.
Ragism.
Tribalism.

The clueless who say, *What doesn't
kill you makes you stronger.*

Your right to use plastic
to buy a frappuccino.

Those who know me
but don't buy my books.

Vanity plates.
Except for:
NO CA CA,
Kvech22 &
IB6UB9.

Paul Janko

Snatched me
a yelping
white
toy-poodle.

He's John
the Revelator
incarnate, but
I call him
Nancy.

Now
we're three:
Nancy, me, and
357
Magnum (worth
every last cent).

So I can splatter
my pained brain
onto the ceiling
if need be.

And blow the
balls off he who
needs to have his
balls blown off.

On the mattress,
357
Magnum, Nancy
& me, watch our
favorite movie:
The Searchers.

John Wayne
doesn't
pretend
his kidnapped
pre-teen niece,
squaw of Comanche
Chief Scar,
is redeemable.

Like me,
he knows
what has been
fucked
cannot be
un-fucked.

The Suspect

Alone in the backseat of the unmarked
cop car, I was still in a state of shock,
when Detective Blarney Stone, who
was riding shotgun, turned and said
something to me; so I couldn't really
hear what it was he said, but could see
that the threads of his bulbous nose
were more purple than red.

Because I had yet to reply, he
again asked, "Do you like to fuck
your girlfriend in the ass?"

I'd been driving to the laundromat
that night, 2 full sacks at my side,
when I found myself surrounded
by wailing sirens and cop cars.
Then I was whisked into one while
my own car was cop-commandeered,
a big scene in my neighborhood. Did
I run a light? No. Hit and run? No.
Had I vowed *never* to be taken alive?

And what of this asshole's
asshole inquiry? I answered
honestly, "I don't have
a girlfriend."

Well-tailored walrus, Detective
Armani Meatball, slammed
the brakes, hard eyed me and said,
"You don't have a girlfriend?"
The 2 masters of my fate gazed
lovingly at one another, as if to say,
He's our man, let the fun begin.

At the eerily unoccupied police
station, they said I could leave
anytime, but we needed to talk
about the mangled dead body
of a girl found on the rooftop of
one of the many 5 story walk-ups
on my block: Front-page killing
that I'd heard and read about.

Was I truly free to leave? Yes.
Why didn't I? From the get-go
they pressed me to let them
into my place, where I'd punched
holes into a door, covered a wall
with news clippings about "Jaws,"
and had drugs. I figured a bleary-
eyed judge might grant a search
warrant. I needed them off me.

Was there a shred of evidence
linking me? No. Did I know
where I was on the night of...?
No. Did I agree to take a ride
downtown for a lie detector
test? Yes. Did I pass the test?
Yes. Did I agree to bite into
wax? Yes. Bite marks match
the killer's? No. Was I questioned
further and kept waiting there
in limbo all night, anyway?
Yes. Was the slightly torn back
seat of my car ripped open,
and the glove compartment
broken into. Yes. The misshapen
sacks meant they'd also rifled
through the dirty laundry,
but that they put back.

Three short lines a year later,
in the Police Blotter section,
of the *New York Daily News,*
the case had been cracked.
The adult son of the old lady
who lived next door to the girl.
The other side of the wall,
to be exact. He didn't live
there, but visited often.

Why me? I'd often have coffee
at the Kingsbridge Diner,
at times drugged-up nodding
into last night's box scores. Deb,
a waitress there, was friendly
with cops who'd stop in. One
must've told her the girl's nose
had been bitten off, because Deb
liked sharing that unreported
horror tidbit. She told me, and I
told her that I knew the victim
from the photo, vaguely recalling
her from back in high school.
Chatty Deb, had shot a bored
finger straight at me.

But fuck me—my car and laundry.
You might need not to believe it,
but what was plain in the air
was that these 2 enforcers of law
couldn't care less. Guilty or innocent,
their only aim, snatching a suspect,
making it stick, rising in rank
and sleeping like babies.

Jack Maurer a/k/a Trigger

You could stroll into the room
anytime Trigger was butt-naked,
getting it on with some stoned
skank. He'd pause and wave his big
hard on. Yet he couldn't piss into
a urinal if anyone was around,
and had to use a stall.

I Should've Helped Him Plot His Escape

Our third floor window faced
the back of another six-story
apartment building. Between
the buildings was a concrete alley.
The building was close enough
so that I could've hit it under-
handed with a Spaldeen. Its sole
balcony was on the second floor.
And although the railed balcony
was as long as that entire side
of the building only one apartment
had access. Through an unpainted
wooden door. The door the woman
would shove the boy out of.

She'd wear a floral apron over her
housecoat and her gray hair tied
tightly in a bun. The boy was about
my age, eight. She looked too old
to be his mother. An otherwise
ordinary looking boy, he was always
dressed up. Slacks, shoes shined,
and a button up short sleeved shirt
in warm weather. A well-scrubbed
little man. Too well scrubbed. I never
saw him on the street. And I never
saw him at school. She'd shove him
out the door, and he'd beg to play
with other kids. Every day, he'd
be left on the balcony—

Alone. No ball. No books. Nothing.
Looking up, down, every which way,
arms at times windmills, he'd pace
and skip for hours. Stopping only
when she'd come out. Stone-faced,

she'd hand him a bowl of mush
and a spoon. But there was nothing
to rest it on. He'd eat standing.

I slid the window open, "Hey!"
I called out to him. He stopped
skipping and looked up at me.
"I'm Ted," I said, and asked
what his name was. "David!"
he shouted excitedly. I invited
him to come out and play. She
must've heard talk and came
bustling out. But when David
pointed to our window and said,
"Look mommy, I made a friend
up there!"—I ducked—and she
dragged him in, screeching
"Mommy will be upset if you
get kidnapped! Mommy will
be upset if you get kidnapped…!"

Getting Some

Thirteen, hair & drawl
like Elvis, his own
back-boned swagger,
he moves to my block
from some distant state.
Within 6 months he makes
out with half the girls in
the neighborhood. Some
a year older than us.
He's asked to play bass
in a local rock band.
Doesn't even plug in.
Why his family moved to—
of all places—the Bronx?
Might have to do with why
he's placed straight into
our grade's class for psychos.
Having never really made
out with a girl on my own,
I'm drawn to the guy. He joins
our crowd. I call for him.

His 12-year-old sister lets
me in. She looks like him,
and although it somehow
comes together better on
her brother, there's nothing
I don't like about her. Kisses
my mouth. Shocks me.
Waves me on to follow—
into her room. *His* sister.
You don't go for a friend's
sister. I stay put in the hall.
He steps out of her room
carrying a girl bride-style.
Both rumpled, but clothed.

Her ass is a nectarine. "She's
a whore," he says. Nods
at me, "Come get some."
"I'm a whore," says the girl,
boldly. His sister yells,
"If my brother & his friend
wanna rape you let 'em."

High Noon at Midnight:
Loomis vs. Mr. Havoc

Laughing his ass off, he spat
on a stylish man walking
a small dog. Then he spat on
the dog. They fled. Raining
close range coughs onto
the back of her head, he
chased a trim gym-bag toting
woman, as she too fled. Havoc
kicked over a street-corner
trash can now, looked into
the 99th Street night and eye-
balled a gangly, bespectacled,
bald guy across the street.

This was Loomis. His arm
around a parking meter as he
nursed a container of coffee.
This decent but tightly-wound
sleepless loner. Juvenile Diabetes.
Thirty-eight. Failing eyesight,
numb feet. Rage! He wanted
a wife & children. Unmoved,
watching the goon carry on,
he readied for violence. High
noon at midnight, Havoc
stomping his way.

Loomis spilled the remaining
coffee onto the street, placed
the container down at the foot
of the parking meter, took 2
steps back onto the middle of
the sidewalk, crossed his arms,
and set his blurry sights on
the oncoming threat. As he took
step one onto the curb, Loomis,
flashing stiff forefingers at him
shouted, "Hey!"

Havoc stopped, eyed Loomis.
Loomis then used his foot to
ghost a line on the sidewalk in
front of where he stood. "Cross
that line… I'm taking an eye!"
Took a step back. Placed his
hands behind him. Up to the line
Havoc stepped—

Stopped.

Eye to eye, an arm's length
apart. Loomis white. Havoc
black. Both were lanky,
and about the same height.
Unlike the much larger black
man who turned the corner—
walking straight into this.

"What's the problem, brother?"
he said to Havoc, handing
him a buck, before adding,
"You best get going."

Trying to downplay the fact
that Loomis had scared him
stiff, Havoc laughed a phony
face-saving laugh, and walked.
His patron moved on.

Loomis was alone.

From a window:
"He's homeless! Crazy!"

"Not crazy enough!" said Loomis.

Old news to me.

Protection

Why would some little kid
spit into my little kid face
for no reason with my father
standing nearby? Not because
he expected to get his head
slammed by an open adult
hand. That same hand then
slammed me. My father not
saying a word to the kid or
me before, during or after.

Later that day the kid's father
called out to us on the street.
He was bigger than my father,
yet he kept his distance and said
something about "Next time you
hit my kid…" Exuding a bring it
on calm, my father said nothing.
I'd never seen him that calm,
surely not when he was beating
my mom or boasting about real
& imagined violence. His calm
unsettled me. Even when he was
seated alone lost in television
his unhinged rage-filled energy
caused my gut to tighten.

I'm unsure if it was before or after
the time my father asked me to step
out of our apartment into the hall
with him to show off his gun by
blasting what he said were blanks
at a wall, but I do know a year
or two had passed since the little
kid spitting episode, because now
around age ten and out on the street

alone, I was in a shoving match
with another kid over who knows what,
when both the kid and his father started
chasing after me. Figuring this grown
man's gonna kick my ass I took off
escaping across an empty lot.

I didn't tell my father about it,
never told him anything about
anything, knew to keep his nasty
scrambled head out of things.
I was protecting him,
my sole inescapable enemy.

Falling

Seated beside me in the front row of the theater's
balcony, my friend said he was frightened by the over-
whelming urge to hurl himself over the low railing.
No joke. He was mired in dread. His eyes though were
not resigned to death. Unclenching my teeth, I let him
know that I'd already imagined myself locked in
a life-or-death clinch with the harmless stranger seated
at my side, and was now frightened that when I stand
a demon in the row behind will calmly shove me.

Where I'm Coming From

Happy to board the retired school bus
turned dollar van just before the driver
said, "No more," I'd have taken any seat
for the hour or so trip. But there were none
left so I resigned myself to getting off,
when the driver got up and led me to
the back where there was a folding chair
that I hadn't seen in the aisle. I wouldn't
have to wait for the next bus. "Oh, I didn't
notice the executive seat," I quipped.
"NOW YOU DID!" shouts a guy seated
in front of me to my left without looking
at me. Damn, I said to myself, that's shut-
the-fuck-up funny shit he unloaded on me.
He rested a heavy hand on his leg. The
leg was spread well into the aisle. It was
the reason why I didn't spot the folding
chair when I first got on.

The scale in my head then tipped from
the funny to the shut-the-fuck-up. He had
taunted me. Like I was some kind of Mr.
Fancy pants. That what I'd said implied
that I was too good for the folding chair.
I'm too good for that entire bus.
But that's not where I was coming from. I
tapped an idiot kid seated next to me on
the shoulder. He took off his headphones
and turned to me. His mouth scowled
but his eyes said curious. Smiling, I said,
"You know I'm sitting in the moneymaking
seat." A stony long moment passed,
then he brightened and said, "Oh, you
mean like it don't really belong here?"
"Yeah," I said, aiming my words at

the back right of my enemy's fat head,
"I don't begrudge these drivers doing
whatever they need to make an extra buck."
But gone were the days I would've added,
"And if not for someone's leg…"

The Gambler

I was playing after school
head-on $1/$2 poker against
my friend Gene's fat gout-
afflicted mother at their place
when the doorbell rang.
"No one else here," I said.
"You want me to get that?"

"Get what?!" she said.

At the door was a handsome
black woman in an ivory,
medium brim church hat.
"My son's in jail," she said.
"But he didn't do anything
I can't forgive him for."

"Can I sleep in his bed?" I asked.

"Yes," she said, fading away.
I shut the door. Got back to
the game, and sat. Gene's
mother was shuffling the deck.

"My mind's not mine," I said.

"Yeah, well I didn't hear no
doorbell," she said. "Anyhow,
you're the same sandbagging
faggot to me. Splash cold water
in your eyes."

"No," I said. "We're about even.
One cut. High card takes all."

"Sure," she said.

And drew a deuce…

I drew the Jack of Hearts.

"HA!" barked Gene, lunging
for the cash. Unnoticed, he'd let
himself in. "You 2 degenerates
are into me for plenty," he said
pocketing what he snatched.

Vesti la Giubba

While I wondered who was more irresistible to women,
Tiger Woods or Pablo Picasso, everyone in the subway car
was suddenly roused by a woman announcing, "I am a
struggling opera singer." That she didn't lead with *sorry
for the interruption* was a plus. I looked up and saw it
wasn't a woman, but a filthy little wisp of a white guy,
his lightly hooded head bowed. "I will sing "*Vesti la giubba*"
from *Pagliacci*," he said. I closed my eyes and allowed myself
to be moved by his subdued and heartfelt tenor. The other
riders were mostly well-dressed young college grads who
flocked to the island of Manhattan, and work very, very
long hours, looking to make their mark and/or to find a mate.
This opera-singing beggar, I knew, didn't have the singing or
begging chops to separate any of these go-getters from a thin
dime. I would seize the compassion-flaunting moment. They
needed to be shown that they were "less than." Led by his
enduringly bowed, hooded head, the singer of opera shuffled
silently through the car. Head to toe, his clothes were once all
white. I reached over and showcased an Abe Lincoln into his open
palm. He didn't say thank you, which was also a plus. Nor did
he call on God to bless me. It wasn't like he had pull with God,
like Tiger Woods or Pablo Picasso.

The Man Who Conquered the World

He married, fathered a boy
& a girl, toiling 7 twelve-hour
days a week behind the wheel
of a NYC cab to make ends
meet. So it was no surprise
he looked tired in the photos
from twenty or so years ago
that his daughter shared at her
wedding party. Months before
the wedding date he'd been fine,
then one day the doctor said
he had lung cancer. His son
& daughter alternated taking
off a week at a time from their
professional lives to be stationed
at his hospital bedside. Sleepless
nights in the nearby recliner. He
died there, but had long since
been fulfilled by how his kids
turned out. This man who years
back had come to scorn his wife
because she ignored or berated
their kids but stayed married
solely to remain under the same
roof as them, caring for & enjoying
his kids, taking off every other
Sunday when they'd tickle
his feet before sunrise rousing
him from much needed sleep.
Happy, he'd get up, loving them
more than he cared for himself.

True Cool

After rolling a thunderous strike to open the game,

Brian Jones haircut-topped Stan Conley rolled 7

more straight to put the heavily betted match away.

Without a word, he then collected his part of the win-

nings from his backslapping backers, kicked off his

rented bowling shoes and slipped back into his black

ankle-length roach killer boots before walking off.

He didn't give a shit about the chance to bowl

a perfect game. Complete in bright red turtleneck he

looked British Invasion, but they said he was a junkie.

Thirteen, I knew that was fucked up, but so what.

Turtles

A kid standing several steps from the man-made lake
was readying to make the running jump onto the large
rock where turtles were lounging. This really bugged me
because it was a given that he was up to no good, and I
like turtles, the way they lazily hang out, don cool armor,
and mind their own fucking business. I was about to say
something to him, but he was with another fourteen or
fifteen year old, and they had a pit bull so I mutely walked
past, continuing my first lap on the paved path around
the lake, stopping a few times to look back, only to see
that the kid has gone from doing shoulder rolls to trunk twists
and back to shoulder rolls. He was posing. I might not have
had the balls to say anything, but he didn't have the balls
to chance that jump. His delay all but assured me that if he
were to give it a go now he'd likely come up soaked or hurt.
Hopefully, he'd crack his head bloody on a rock. His body
left afloat in the lake overnight, like that of a turtle I'd seen
the day before. A turtle that I'm sure didn't die a natural death.

I'd understand if there were girls around. He'd show the girls
how he could fly, show them a turtle up close, but there weren't
any girls around. More likely he was the kind who drowned
stray cats. I could also understand if there was a sheep
on the rock and he wanted to hump it, but it was a turtle.
I may be a straight male but that doesn't mean I'm inter-species
love phobic. Okay, so he's an every boy daredevil. I get it.
But really, like everything else, it all comes back to yours truly.

Teenage boys and pit bulls always bring me down. Turtles
lift my spirits. I kept walking. And distracted myself reading
official signs: Welcome to Hudson County Nature Trails at
North Hudson Park, Keep off Lake Thin Ice, and Trout Stocked
Water Woodcliff Lake (stapled to a tree), sidestepping people
who simply because they could were using their cell phones
to take pictures of one another. While slob fishermen sat on
folding chairs, hands free, next to their multiple rod set ups.

Upon completing the first of my 3 or 4 almost mile-long laps
around the lake, back to what I'll call turtle rock, I see the same
fucking kid holding a turtle. "I see you worked up the nerve
to make the jump," I say. "I hope you're gonna put that turtle back."
"Yeah," he says. "I wouldn't do anything to hurt the turtle."
Pleased with myself and feeling hopeful, I walked on. I unzipped
my hip sack and took out my large padded headphones and tiny
ipod, listening only through one ear to stave off the tinnitus
that had begun in the other. My mood had cooled so I started
with a mellow but soulful mix of artists like Glen Campbell,
Dionne Warwick, and The Carpenters... After Campbell's sweet
and melancholy "Wichita Lineman," came Karen Carpenter's
"Rainy Days and Mondays Always Bring Me Down," but like I
said, teenage boys and pit bulls always bring *me* down, so I
thumbed a Lester Young playlist on my ipod and lost myself
in his melodic airborne sax. When I reached turtle rock after
my third lap the kid, his friend, and dog were no longer there.
A woman holding a little girl's hand stood by, telling her,

"Because the turtle is upside down." So that's what that funky
looking fleshy thing that I'd seen before was, a turtle on its back.
The kid had flipped the turtle on its back. Funny thing though,
I'd noticed that turtle on its back before he was on the scene,
but had my distance Ray Bans on and the sky had turned gray,
so I didn't know what I was looking at. It could've been anything
from a human brain or intestines to a live giant vagina. But I knew
that the kid had to have something to do with it.

With every step, I was getting more and more pissed. When I was his age
I know I could've made that same running jump. But back then I didn't
give a rat's ass about turtles. I needed to get into *the zone*. Like when I
was the only kid who was able to throw the ball through the tire hole
from shallow left field on day one of little league tryouts, or when I hand-
snatched a horsefly mid-air. I knew I'd get both of those feats done right
before I did them. I needed to access the zone to make the running jump,
and set the turtle upright. Or fuck myself up trying… Or maybe I could
find a really long branch. Fuck the branch. Bent on making the jump I
began the march back to Turtle Rock, but suddenly realized that you
can't channel the zone, the zone channels you. So I did the next best
thing, looping the Sturm und Drang of Black Sabbath's "War Pigs," to
psych myself to fever pitch. I was a commando. Spotting the two boys
and their dog in the not too far off park, I thought of calling out to them,
telling the kid that maybe he could make the jump again and undo what
someone did. But no, this was on me. War Pigs. Hello death.

When I got there the upside down turtle was gone! This was truly a miracle. I wouldn't have to give up my body. Vital, since I was now aware that even if I made the running jump onto the rock, I'd need to make the same jump back without a running start. A feat the kid couldn't do either. That's when I saw that there were 2 large rocks inches below the water line. The kid likely took off his sneakers, rolled up his pants, and stepped over to snag a turtle. I was right all along. The posing kid didn't have the balls. I could've done the same. Flummoxed, I wondered how an upside down turtle could get off a rock. It was by the edge of the rock. Had one or more of the other turtles nudged the upside-downer into the water? Hell no, that was wishful thinking. I needed to know. An elderly couple walked towards me, the woman clutching a pair of large brown stuffed animals against her chest. The husband seemed embarrassed. I made sure not to stare at them, needlessly fiddling with my headphones instead. A bunch of imbeciles passed before I stopped a power-walker, filled him in, and asked if he'd seen anything. "It's hard to believe," he said. "But what you saw was a turtle that has only the rim of its shell. He's very spunky and basks among the others on that rock most days." "Wow!" I say. How could the shell come off? Nodding towards the lake, he says, "Who knows what goes on down there? "Not me" I say. "But I sure as shit know what goes on up here."

House Call

Hadn't seen Duke in over
twenty years, but last night
we knew each other as soon
as our paths crossed in Penn
Station. So I got to ask him
about something I'd heard
way back. Had to do with his
beer truck driver father,
who named him for former
Brooklyn Dodger great Duke
Snider, and often stood on
the top stoop of their walk-up,
smoking a cigar, and keeping
an eye on kids playing street
games. Kids like runty Ira Fox
who lived in the flat below them,
and would stickball-bat-clang
the steam pipes to signal he
was coming up to visit. Was it
true that when young hot shot
heart surgeon Dr. Ira Fox showed
up in the old neighborhood
to visit his mother, your father
made him give him a check-up
on the top stoop? Duke said
yeah. Ira leapt 2 steps at a clip.
and nodded hello, looking to fly
by Duke & his father, but Duke's
father stepped in front of him
and raised his palm for Ira to stop,
and unbuttoning his Hawaiian
shirt so Ira could ear-to-chest
check his bare chest. He checked
his pulse, too. "Good!" said Ira.
"Foxy," said Duke, "don't forget
how my dad looked out for you
if he ever needs cuttin' up."

Mercy

"Meeting on the internet and the thousand-
plus miles distance between us added
to the allure. He was 28. I'm already 35.
The first weekend we met in the flesh
was nothing but bliss. But, I ended up
pregnant. No, neither of us planned on that.
Having endured a childhood spent shuffled
among foster homes, he wanted to make
it right. He proposed marriage. I happily
accepted. After all, don't I deserve a family
of my own? On day 2 of his 2 day drive
to the ceremony, the engine of his car
broke down. We rescheduled the marriage.
In the interim I miscarried. I was shattered.
He was a comfort, said, together, we'd see
it through. The next day, he calls the whole
thing off. My mom said to pretend the whole
thing never happened. The therapist said
there are no quick fixes. Really, I don't feel
like living anymore. I still can't believe it."
I assure her, "The baby was unborn to spare
you from a lifetime of marital misery." I don't
believe it, but no one can say for sure it's a lie.
And if it happened tomorrow, I'd say it again.

Thrilla in Manila

Whites had long since fled
the Bronx's Grand Concourse
leaving me, the sole guy at
the Loews Paradise theater
for the live, big screen showing
of the "Thrilla in Manila" who
wasn't Black or Puerto Rican.
And no, that didn't make me
uptight. Being expected to know
formal dining etiquette, that
would've made me uptight.

Among the first to gain entrance,
I took an aisle seat & a swig
from my fifth of Smirnoff vodka.
Someone tapped my shoulder,
a powerful looking guy behind
me wanting some. He was already
rocking & after throwing back
a prodigious swig of mine he laughed
& laughed, while repeating, "I'm
crippled for life." He was an ox,
but his self-assessment was fine
by me. Fixed on his mantra we
laughed on through round one.
Then he disappeared.

The crowd was roaring 50/50
Frazier/Ali. *You* thought they
would be wildly Ali? What do
you know? Me, I hoped the fight
would beat the hype, "Smokin'
Joe" & "The Greatest," delivering.
I wanted to witness history.

Every inch as valiant as Achilles,
Smokin' Joe Frazier sat on his stool
after his trainer threw in the towel.
The clash had been epic. I emptied
the bottle, someone passed me a joint,
the place stayed raucous, and if that ain't
inner-city you can kiss my ass.

The Rise & Fall of Billy Horst

When Teresa walked past the street
corner where we were hanging out
you shouted, "Slut!" and tossed
pennies at her feet. This confused me.
After all, you said that you *balled* her.
And although I'd never heard anyone
say balled before I knew it had to
be some kind of sex act conquest,
so why would you be mad at her?
But I dared not ask. A boy, I figured,
should be born knowing all that stuff.
And not only did you know stuff,
you had the baffling gift of gab,
shooting the shit with all walks of
life as though you shared a history.

No surprise you became a lawyer,
making tons of money, separating
insurance companies from some of
their loot. You could afford all vices
known to man times ten, and tuck wife
and kids away in a leafy cul-de-sac.

When Dix's car was wrecked, rear-
ended on the Cross Bronx, I advised
him to call you. Since he wasn't badly
injured, you took on the open-and-shut
case "only as a favor for an old friend."
Tapped out, Dix was keenly aware
that this business could go on forever.
Still, he was pleased.

I was in the lobby of a club in Yonkers,
where Felix Cavaliere was featured,
when I ran into her. "Teresa?" I asked.
She talks marriage, kids, divorce,

remarriage, and before I could utter
another word, says she was "a stick
with small tits," an only child of older
parents. Then, after you'd gained their
trust, you went and tore off her blouse,
tried to rape her. You stayed pissed
because she fought you off.

Forever came. You lost the case for Dix.
Zero. Shattered, he called me. I called
you, and was blown off, "I never liked
the guy," you said. "Anyway, he always
was full of shit." Dix had trusted you,
but when the shock of *zero* eased some,
Dix coldly reviewed the case, showing
many instances of gross mishandling to
me. He said you'd sold him out to get
a quick payout from the same insurance
company on a big money case. Having
steered him to his unmaking, I felt tainted.
But Dix never held it against me. He
married, moved out west, and turned
himself into a big success.

Try as he would Dix couldn't shake
the hatred he carried for you. Never
could forget how you buried him.
Figuring sleaze like you had to have
enemies, he hired a detective to look
into your ever-thriving practice.

For about the same amount you'd spend
on a high-end hooker, he was informed
you'd set up a hospital x-ray tech hot line.
Illegal, but you wanted an edge. A tech
who wasn't on your payroll felt left out.

And as Dix laughingly says, he "dropped
a dime." You fought the case and lost.
Didn't serve time but were disbarred.
Last I heard you were trying to make
a buck as a go-between, selling a painting.
Then you were dead.

No Reason Why

Looking down at the sickly orange liquid and jagged
shards of glass on the sidewalk, I damn well know
that if the bottle of orange soda tossed from a window
of a tall apartment building had landed a foot to the left
it would've exploded on top of my head. Sprawled in
a puddle of blood, I'd be too dead to be embarrassed
about being the sole winner of this lottery of the unlucky.
When a passerby calls the cops, I split,

and take shelter in the scrap paper chicken scratch
I pull from a back pocket: barber, bank, supermarket,
haircut, withdraw sixty bucks at Bank of America,
and buy a quarter pound of capicola ham, smoked turkey,
and a 3-pack of roach motels at Gristedes. Less than
an hour later, having completed all missions, I crumple
the list, and chuck it into a street corner garbage can.

Home, I place one trap below the kitchen sink, the other
2 on the bathroom floor, below the sink, and behind
the toilet. I'd rather swallow a roach than have one crawl
into my accessible asshole while I'm trying to take a shit.
Lunching on the smoked turkey, I ask myself who
it was who'd toss an unopened bottle of orange soda onto
a bustling street. I figure, a punk kid acting on a whim.
Although, for all I know it might've dropped out of the sky.

I then retrace my steps leading to my brush with death.
Did anything happen to throw off the timing of my move-
ments, thusly saving me from death? Someone on the street
bump me breaking my stride? Did a stranger stop me to ask
for the time? Was this an instance when the spirit of my late
mother intervened to save my life? I think not. And I'm not
grand or guarded enough to believe the close call had anything
to do with God. Yet, I know the small still voice within.

After Waiting for the Soldiers to Go Away

I walked past the corpses.
Scattered corpses littered
the street. Many times
before, I had come upon
such scenes. A small corpse
caught my eye. It was that
of a cat. Down on one knee,
I shut its yellow eyes.

Donna

Living on top of Wah's Chinese
laundry, they were Polish. Her
older brother looked Puerto Rican.
We called him "Spanish Eddie."
She was flat and skinny with lush,
straight, dark-blond hair flowing
well past her waist. Could've been
Rapunzel, but she talked like a guy.
We hung out in the same crowd
by the corner Carvel. She'd laugh
heartily at my wisecracks, and like
me, favored The Rolling Stones
and hated the world. I'd reassure
her: Nobody blamed her for Spanish
Eddie's suspected part in setting up
a neighborhood pot dealer for
a home-invasion-gunpoint-robbery.
Seventeen, she took no breaks
between lousy boyfriends. She
dumped the latest, a puppy-dog-eyed
snake (whose name I never cared
to remember) after he stole a roll
of quarters she'd stashed in the sock
drawer of the dresser by her bed.
Next day, it was just me and Donna,
smoking a joint, lounging in the back
seat of a friend's wreck. Her hair—
it struck me—was far better than any
tits, eyes, or ass. Hot and heavy—
when she abruptly pulls away. Says,
"We can't, we're friends." "Oh," I say,
"you mean like you just wanna be
friends?" "No," she says, "it's just
that we *are* friends."

For What It's Worth

As soon as the rock & roll
show at Young Israel
Synagogue ended, the 4
of us 13-year-old boys left.
Same stark synagogue where
me and one of the other boys,
Jules, were Bar Mitzvahed
the month before and said to
have become men. The rest
of the audience had gone
home, and we were now
hanging out right across
the street in the cold snowy
1967 Bronx winter's night.

Our heads buzzing in awe
after experiencing the Chambers
Brothers blast off and into
"The Time Has Come Today"
through stacked Marshall amps.
And my soul has been
psychedelicized.

The fresh-faced cowboys
with cute haircuts, who
closed the show, and surely
came from places where
there were wide open spaces,
now stood across the street
waiting on their ride. They
were supposed to be cool,
but they weren't loud enough,
didn't rock and the hippie
thing hadn't oozed in
from the suburbs yet.

One of our firmly packed
snowballs hit their blond
front man with the bushy
sideburns square on his natty
tan cowboy hat. If it had been
the nonpareil Neil Young
or Richie Furay who got hit
I'd be ashamed to tell it,
but I can't say I give a damn
about Stephen Stills and who-
ever it was who played drums
for Buffalo Springfield. Stills
& the drummer, both tearing
ass, chased us down the block.

When we got to the corner
the other 3 boys turned
right. They were lightning
and I wasn't, but I was cagey
so I veered left, and quickly
disappeared into a dark alley.

The next day, sharkskin suit
wearing stud, Jules, who'd
chanted his Bar Mitzvah
recital in tongues instead
of Hebrew, because he didn't
care about making his mother
happy, said the 2 Buffalos
who chased them were real
fast, tough to shake.

Tonight I'm at BB King's
waiting to hear Richie Furay
perform on his 70th birthday.

Minister Furay. Audience
friendly, Richie comes over
to our table, places his right
hand on my man Tony's
shoulder and asks if it's okay
to invoke a blessing. Rob
had told Richie that Tony
was facing heart surgery. I let
the wacky thought of asking
Richie about that long ago
cold snowy winter's night pass
as I watch hard-headed lapsed
Catholic Tony bow his head,
accept Richie's blessing
because he loves his music
much more than he rejects
Jesus. Elated from witnessing
the benediction, I am as close
to ready as I may ever get
to kick up my heels at tonight's
barn dance hoe down.

Ambrus Bohn

Hateful, small & manic, he was known as Bone, and fancied
himself a basketball player. Unable to drive to the hoop
effectively, or to pull up off his dribble for a jump shot,
he'd dribble-on aimlessly by the top of the key, and was a pesky
crafty butcher on D. More distinctively, in a cracked concrete
schoolyard of rusted rims, he had the foulest mouth.
His curious mantra: Eat me, eat me, eat me...

The Message

Had I known it would cost 5 times more
for me to get to the Long Island library
to do the poetry reading than what I'd make
from that night's sale of 3 copies of my book
I'd have done it anyway. Libraries are holy.
The neighborhood I grew up in didn't have
one. What kind of neighborhood doesn't have
a library? You tell me. What kind of a library
has a nearly non-existent poetry section? Most
all of them nowadays. The red light flashes
on my answering machine. I press play…

Muted message: male voice, my reading,
please call… Alright! No one's calling
just to say hi you suck. Who knows?
A patron of the arts? A top publisher?
A fan offering pure cocaine? More likely,
the caller was a host of a reading who'd ask
me to feature. Maybe an editor requesting
poems for their journal. I'd return this gift
call after coffee, tomorrow morning.

Despite the message being muted, his phone
number was strangely clear. I dialed. He said
he'd seen in a local newspaper, that I was a poet
who'd read at a library, not too far from his
bookshop. "Who am I talking to?" I asked.
"Lou," he said, rolling into how he'd acquired
a fine poetry collection, but was having no luck
stirring up interest, so last night he called me
to ask if I wanted to buy it. Dejected, I said,
"No. Most public libraries have less than one
shelf of poetry. What *we* have has no value."

Teeth

In another time, in another place, he'd have been a kosher butcher
or a cobbler, but stubby-fingered Dr. Abelman was an oral surgeon.
Today, as I sit in his dental chair awaiting his appearance, my mind's
eye is forever locked on an image of him wielding a meat cleaver.
As soon as he walks in, he says, "This visit we complete your implants,
but before we do we always get paid in full." I'm a bit taken aback
because, although I expected a demand for the seven thousand dollars
I owe to be made today, I didn't expect it to fly out of Abelman's mouth.
I expected it would come from his attractive but steely receptionist,
or one of his in-house billers. He then adds, "After this, you won't have
to see me again." As if that in itself would be reason enough for me
to max out my Amex. Although, considering the needlessly torturous
ordeal he'd put me through, it probably was. Savoring the chance to
utter the four letter word, I say, "I've got *cash*." The promise of cash,
and the fact that I was already seated, moved him to complete the work.
Afterwards, I went to the reception area to pay. Somehow, he was already
there. Five or six feet behind the reception desk and facing a side wall
of file cabinets, the employer of two full-time clerks stood atop a stepstool
casually thumbing through an open drawer, the corner of his eye fixed
on me. I pulled out a wad of cash, snapping twenty tens, one at a time,
and handed the meager two hundred dollars to his receptionist, who now
cracked an I-don't-give-a-fuck-about-you-but-am-glad-you're-fucking-
with-him smile. Abelman turned toward me. He didn't wield a meat cleaver,
but looked so right in a butcher's apron. Blood smeared red.

2 Kennedys

As the station wagon began to pull away, ten year-old me chased after it, extending my hand to the lean and polished, wavy-brown-haired Bobby Kennedy who stood on its flat top and leaned down to shake my hand, firmly. No one else was close by. He had just finished stumping on the Bronx corner of Fordham & Valentine. His kindness toward me made me feel that there were great men in the world. Men who cared about others, men like his brother, The President who was killed 2 short years ago. I held fast to my encounter with him, keeping it secret to keep it holy.

Three years later, he too was killed. I was rattled, but imagined that other great men would step in and somehow make it all right. I ate the cream cheese and jelly sandwich my mom placed before me, just as I did 5 years earlier after our third-grade teacher had dismissed us, upon hearing the principal's muffled words echo from the box speaker mounted high on the front wall of our class-room. Regal and forever-dead, John F. Kennedy's visage adorned more walls in Catholic-owned stores than that of Jesus Christ.

truths & other lies

say
your gym
teacher makes
you workout,

sweat a stink
dress again,

and next class
is the one time
per week you
sit beside

the girl who
rock 'n' rolls
your heartbeat,

you must lie.
forge a doctor's
note to stay
out of gym.

true love
trumps
squat thrusts.

=

say
you're a juror,
a kid drug
dealer's on
trial, you know
the worst of

the worst

thieves thrive
behind the great
wall of too
big to fail,

you get an okay
feeling about
the kid.

truth is
I deem him
too small to
fail, he ain't
taking your fall.

=

say
the man now
hiding behind
your couch
is on the run,

a rabid mob's
out to nab him,

you know
he didn't do
what he's said
to have done.

they're knock—
        knock—
        knocking—
on your door,

lusting to do
what rabid
mobs do.

you must lie.
say, he's not here.

=

greater truths
are often clear.

What Mattered Most

On and on my 5th grade
teacher Miss O'Gorman
gushed to mom saying
how fast I'd read *Jason
and the Golden Fleece.*

That most of my classmates
also could've done it
didn't matter
it was me she chose
a son of Jews 'just off the boat'
the handsomest boy in class
who quietly stood by his
modestly nodding
delighted mom.

My mom
who wished me 'pleasant dreams' nightly, mornings
served me tummy-warming crunchy French toast, who
wiped my 7-year-old ass when I got home from the hospital
after surgery to excise crippling rectal cysts, made sure I
never wore hand-me-downs, called me Tadeuszu,
protected me from hexes,

and who'd be dead
before I reached puberty.

My loving and gentle mom

who escaped the Nazis
only to marry a monster
who fathered me.

And I'd like to say her happiness
at that 5th grade parents/teachers meeting
even then
mattered more to me
than my puffed out chest—

But I'd be lying.

Biography of Blood Fouler

In the middle of eluding
genocide, he stopped
to set a farmhouse on fire—
after snapping the farmer's
neck, killing him. He'd worked
for the man, in the no-name
Latvian village where they lived.
Its straw-roof burst into flames
all at once. He'd say, the farmer
had bothered his sister.
No doubt he'd witnessed
someone snap another's neck.
At 14 though, he wasn't up
to snapping any robust peasant's
neck. Never cared for anyone
outside of himself. Whether
the farmer was burned
alive is anyone's guess.

In the new world,
his 13-year-old son taught
him the game of baseball.
He taught the boy how to tie
his own shoelaces and to smash
what you can't easily fix. His
9-year-old daughter talked him out
of his dumb plan for petty larceny.
He taught her rote multiplication
and abandoned her on the NYC
subway. The boy's bladder
was wrecked. The girl's hair fell
out. Both kids knew dad was blah
blue the old black birdy. He spoke
7 languages but had no friends.
When asked why he murdered
the mother of his children,
he'd say, "I did that?"

advice to my unborn son

if someone comes
to you with *the truth*
run

brush with baking soda
drink vodka straight
kick low
punch high
floss floss floss

find a job you don't hate

to deter a bully
saw stickball bat
in half
hide in bushes
flash attack
mercilessly

don't worry
pray
same shit

go to prom
escort homeliest
girl most likely to
recall it fondly

never watch sports
play
those guys
don't know
you're alive

any man named tim
             tom
             ted

who refers to himself as timmy
                            tommy
                            teddy
will steal the eyeballs
out your head and/or make
monkey love with your woman

eat no more than
2 meals a day

don't attempt to
handicap the ponies
analyze tote board
and follow
the smart money

tip starbuck's baristas
remember salvatore allende
stay away from girls named la la
never command anyone to
have a nice day

treat people the way
you'd like to be treated

if all else fails
become born again or hassid

make believe
you believe
better yet
if you do

The Love Fest Will Begin

Shrink touted Wall Street & Thorazine, but into poetry I fell.
Roll my words on concrete, our world spins in the sky.
A friend says the love fest will begin when I'm dead.

Snatched Shrink's pipe from his mouth, smashed it on my head.
Ink spilt on an empty page is a black cat streaking by.
Shrink touted Wall Street & Thorazine, but into poetry I fell.

An orange is to a guitar as a tangerine is to a mandolin.
In the beginning was the word, before the word became a lie.
A friend says the love fest will begin when I'm dead.

"I need a man to show me life," Maria said.
I had no reply.
Shrink touted Wall Street & Thorazine, but into poetry I fell.

Saul took a fall, got up, was Paul said, "For our sins Jesus bled."
Limp in the jaws of a low-flying bat a rabbit's devoured alive.
A friend says the love fest will begin when I'm dead.

Snatched shrink's pipe from his mouth, smashed it on his head.
Everything matters, but there is no reason why.
Shrink touted Wall Street & Thorazine, but into poetry I fell.
A friend says the love fest will begin when I'm dead.

White Knuckles

The past is the past, but it's always present
—Olga Maria Rodriguez Farinas

Twelve-year-old twin sisters Emily and Nan were away
at summer camp when their parents were slain in a suburban
home invasion robbery. The sisters were whisked from camp
by their kindly godparents, who raised them in the same
community, where they too, owned a home. Although each girl
had her own separate friends, they got along fine and shared
a powerful and consoling silent bond. At school, they continued
to excel. Occasionally, an adult or a kid would point and whisper,
cutting deep, all others seemed comfortable with the unspoken
taboo on the subject. The sisters went on to different colleges
out-of-state, where they married, lived, and had families
of their own. They did not, however, maintain any contact.

Dream Fisher

Dad tied a string to
a random stick, handed
it to me and said kid go
fish, before casting his
rod into the quiet,
steady country river.
OK by me. My Bronx
eyes, ears & heart
were flooded by the river.
I never cared to hook
a helpless flopping fish.

Back on the block
I could jerry-rig
a rod from discarded
wire hangers to fish
Spaldeens out of sewers
or work the wires
to lift a condemned
drenched & crying
cat from the sewer,
as the Clausen sisters
cheered blonde delight.

But neither Clausen
sister has ever appeared
in my dreams. Nor have
flopping fish, crying
cats or sewers, and every-
thing about my old man
was a nightmare.

Over & over, I dream
of walking a secret
path through the woods
to that river. Always,
blissfully alone.

Geometry

After handing out the test, our geometry teacher
the dreamy but serious Miss Martin gave out
chewing gum. That Juicy Fruit Friday afternoon
she stood up front and I found myself staring
at her. The crippling need to repeatedly order
random words and numbers 24/7 within my head,
eased. "Why're you staring, Ted?" she quietly
asked before the entire class. Clutching that rare
untormented moment, I didn't feel awkward
but stopped staring and shut my eyes. I got a zero—
I was too grateful released from being a hostage
to my own head to wrestle a hypotenuse. Since
the zero was an aberration, at the end of the term
she tossed it. But what I really wanted was to lay
my pained head on her shoulder and learn to cry.

The Mexican

Ahead of the crowd, I settle into a choice window seat.
This former school bus won't roll from Times Square
deep into New Jersey until every seat is paid for. I eye
all those boarding. They are, to quote Sly Stone,
everyday people. More than a few women board, lugging
shopping bags and little kids, and despite knowing
they will have to put their bags or kid on their laps,
they spread out as though ready to picnic. If I'm looking
for a seat, and need to ask one of these women to kindly
reign in her domain, I get pissed off. If I'm already seated,
I make damn sure my things are on the floor at my feet
or on my lap. Legs slightly apart, I will not budge
for any man. Always there are a number of larger than
normal (yes, normal)-sized boarders, and if you need
to sit beside one, or worse yet, beside a legs-way-spread
motherfucker, half of you painfully ends up in the aisle,
where you're sure to be mauled by fat asses, and battered
by bag after bag, at every one of the 10,000 New Jersey
stops. When a rare, slim, maybe sweet smelling woman
looks for a seat, I shrink, to make the spot beside me more
inviting. It never works. A regular-sized guy ends up
sitting beside me. The last person allowed to board
is a small, taut Mexican laborer. When he finds no place
to sit, he heads back to the driver to retrieve his fare
and leave. The driver, though, accounts for every seat,
and knows there's one remaining. He rises and waves
the Mexican on, escorting him to a woman seated beside
her small child, a woman who, moments ago, had seen
the Mexican looking for a seat, but hadn't made any
move to put her big-headed kid on her lap. Coldly,
the driver gestures for her to do so. As she lifts her kid,
the driver turns to the Mexican, but he's no longer there.
Silently, he's stepped to the rear of the bus, where he stands.
The driver gets back behind the wheel. The Mexican exudes
a kind of detached peacefulness, like a turtle sunning
on a rock. Everything I never learned about being a man,
I learn from that Mexican, this late afternoon, on that bus.

About the Author

Ted Jonathan is a poet and short story writer. Born and raised in the Bronx, he now lives in New Jersey. His poems and stories have appeared in many magazines and anthologies. Translations of his work have appeared in Russian magazines. He's been nominated for a Pushcart Prize twice. His chapbook *Spiked Libido* was published by Neukeia Press. His full-length collection of poems and short stories, *Bones & Jokes,* was published by NYQ Books (2009).